PROMOTING COMMUNITY MENTAL HEALTH
—— IN ——
GUYANA:

A Resource Guide for Practitioners

Sharlene Voogd Cochrane
Marjorie A. Jones
Catherine Koverola

ISBN: 978-1-4834-7168-6 (sc)
ISBN: 978-1-4834-7169-3 (e)

Lulu Publishing Services rev. date: 07/20/2017

Table of Contents

Acknowledgments

Thank you to the many groups and individuals who made this partnership and this publication possible:

The Government of Guyana
Ministry of Social Services
Minister and Officers of the Ministry of Education

UNICEF Guyana

Lesley University Administration
Dean, Faculty, and Staff of the Graduate School of Arts and Social Sciences

Lesley University Trustee, Carol Moriarty, who generously funded the book's publication

The Graduates of the Lesley University/Guyana Degree Program
Stephen Bactawar
Juanita Cameron
Oslyn Crawford
Sharon Dyall
Priscilla Gonsalves
Haimraj Hamandeo
Lotoya Hilliman
Kaycina Jardine
Onika Pearson
Sewpaul Persaud
Vickchand Ramphal
Anand Sharma
Azharuddin Ahmad Rahat Zahaur

Introduction

This book serves as a resource guide for practitioners, counselors, child protection workers, and human service professionals in Guyana and throughout the Caribbean who seek to promote community mental health in their unique cultural contexts. It draws upon the learning and experience of thirteen Guyanese professionals who completed an Interdisciplinary Master of Arts degree through Lesley University in 2014, focused on trauma sensitive assessment and intervention for children, families, and communities.

Each of the graduates of the Lesley University/Guyana Degree Program completed a final project focused on a particular population and topic, researching and analyzing the issue and developing and presenting a workshop for colleagues or clients. Throughout the book their voices and experiences apply new understandings and skills to work in varied contexts within Guyana. The book provides practical real life examples of community mental health promotion by dedicated professionals committed to making a difference.

The Lesley University/Guyana Degree Program students,
Dr. Marjorie A. Jones, and Dr. Catherine Koverola before
the Ministry of Education, Georgetown, Guyana

Intended to serve as a guide for practitioners of many backgrounds, particularly for those who work with people around issues of violence and trauma, such as educators, clergy and law enforcement, it is not a guidebook on how to provide therapy and counseling. Our book focuses on how to provide resources to individuals, families and communities from a psycho-educational context that is informed by an understanding of trauma. The workshops and processes we discuss are designed to educate professional colleagues about mental health practices and related cultural issues, rather than direct therapeutic or clinical sessions. We underscore the importance of referring individuals who could benefit from therapy to appropriately trained clinicians.

Chapter I: Intersections of Culture and Trauma with Practitioner Reflections

This chapter examines the crucial role of the complexity of culture in our understanding of community mental health. We draw upon the lived experiences of Guyanese practitioners to provide assessments of learning related to promoting culturally responsive community mental health.

Chapter II: Community Mental Health: Strategies for Increasing Capacity

This practical guide provides planning and strategies for delivering a psycho-educational workshop, paying close attention to cultural relevance.

Chapter III: Sample Workshops Promoting Community Mental Health

Developed by human service practitioners, the chapter presents a broad range of community based mental health outreach options that can be utilized in a variety of contexts in order to engage with colleagues and respond to clients who have experienced trauma.

Chapter IV: Sustainability: Self Care for the Practitioner

Explores the concept of "vicarious trauma" and provides recommendations on how to ensure the health and vitality of practitioners by maintaining a practice of self-care and connections.

Chapter V: Background on Lesley University/ Guyana Trauma Training Partnership

The historical backdrop for the partnership developed by Lesley University, UNICEF Guyana, and the Government of Guyana. The partnership forms the basis of this Guide.

Chapter I. Intersections of Culture and Trauma in the Development of Psycho-educational Community Based Services

Overview

We invite you to join us in examining the complexity of culture as we consider its importance in understanding psycho-educational service delivery in Guyana. Such services are provided in educational situations such as conferences, department meetings, and group sessions with parents, educators, and colleagues, where the facilitator's goal is to educate the group about aspects or skills in community mental health. These experiences may make use of counseling and therapeutic skills; however these are not clinical situations, they are not therapy.

Culture plays an important role in such psycho-educational gatherings. In a Ted Talk, Charlie Hartwell said, "We listen with our ears but hear with our hearts" (2011). Hearing with our hearts leads to understanding. When we approach a complex problem or issue with deep understanding we are able to respond wisely and compassionately. Often well-meaning individuals who truly want to do good in fact cause harm because they do not have the understanding of the context and what might be truly helpful. This can be the case in multi-cultural contexts where individuals make faulty assumptions about others and act upon them without a deep intercultural understanding. These assumptions often become attenuated in the face of trauma and crisis situations, leading to responses and interventions that may further isolate and alienate the very individuals and communities one is hoping to support.

Understanding Culture

As we embark on examining how to promote community mental health within a cultural context, let us look at the question of "What is Culture?" The concept of culture can be defined as a complex network of knowledge, beliefs, values, and customs shared by members of society. Such a network includes the many aspects of our individual and group identity, such as race, ethnicity, religion, gender, language, and class. As Rosen (2014) explains "culture is the values, beliefs, attitudes, and norms that shape, unite, and characterize the world view and behavior of individuals within a particular group." (p. 156).

Learning about the varieties of cultural networks of clients or students is critical to serving those populations. Practitioners also need to be aware of their own cultural identity and assumptions, as well as that of the individuals and specific communities that they serve. Developing cultural responsiveness requires awareness of one's personal reactions and attitudes about cultural bias and beliefs, as well as curiosity and knowledge about others and specific skills in interacting across cultures.

All cultures have established norms about interpersonal relationships, gender roles and hierarchy, communication, and family and community boundaries. For example, in many cultures it is an established practice to keep all family business within the family. If there is a problem in the family, one sorts it out within the family and it is not appropriate or acceptable to share the information outside the family unit. In such a cultural milieu it would be unacceptable for a family member to share about family violence with an outsider.

Therefore, seeking help in a case of domestic violence would be a violation of the cultural norms and the mere attempt to seek outside intervention could initiate an unfortunate silencing and further victimization of the individual reaching out for help. It is critical for those endeavoring to develop and provide effective intervention strategies for situations, such as domestic violence, to understand the cultural context. Having good intentions is simply not sufficient and in fact can cause irreparable harm.

Another important aspect of culture is that it is not static; rather, it is ever evolving, in terms of cultural norms, values, and understandings. While there are overarching aspects of any given culture, there can also be great heterogeneity within what an outsider might assume is a given cultural norm. So we turn now to consider Guyanese culture.

Kaieteur Falls, Guyana

Historical Context

Guyana is often called the Land of Six Peoples, including Afro-Guyanese, (descendants of enslaved Africans), Indo-Guyanese (descents of indentured East Indian laborers), Indigenous Amerindians, and smaller numbers of Chinese, Portuguese, and Europeans. The circumstances of arrival for each of the groups and their subsequent experiences have shaped both the culture of the respective groups and the Guyanese culture as a whole. Given a long period as an English colony, a tumultuous period of enslavement, and an economic history of sugar cane and rice production, Guyana shares similar cultural and historical bonds with its Caribbean neighbors.

The rich demographic reality in Guyana reflects the number of racial/ethnic groups, social class dynamics, gender and kinship relations, religious diversity, and geography, including differences in urban and rural resources. The variety indicates the necessity for mental health professionals and intervention methods responding to violence, inequality, and trauma to reflect the particular cultural contexts of individual practitioners and clients.

When considering the influential impact of British colonialism upon contemporary cultural systems in Guyana there is a noted orientation around the idea of 'difference.' This can be seen in the post-colonial retention of historically rooted conflation of race, class, cultural boundaries, and social hierarchies that sustained the British imperial "ethos" over enslaved Africans, Indian laborers, and other forced migratory groups from "state aided immigration and indenture" (Seecharan, 1997, p.130 and 136). Today post-colonial Guyana can be described as a "politics of cultural struggle," specifically the politicized racialization of Afro-Guyanese, Indo-Guyanese, and 'racialized othered groups' such as Indigenous Amerindians (Trotz, 2003, p 5-6).

This contemporary "politics of difference" imposed from Guyana's former colonial history has visibly influenced systems of gender, kinship relations, cultural practices, and ideas of labor. For example, despite the rich ethnic diversity in Guyana there are low rates of inter-racial relationships, especially marriages between African and Indian descent Guyanese groups (Trotz, 2003, pg. 21). In terms of gender relations, regionally based scholarship has shown that differences in gender roles can be demarcated by ethnic group differentiation. Afro-Guyanese households are often found to be female-headed and matrifocal, yet women have false dominance as they live under patriarchal structures and male providers. Indo-Guyanese households often reflect early-age arranged marriages with a sense of male authority and female submissiveness (Trotz, 2003, p 6-8, 14-15). In terms of violence against women, cultural ideals can often be found to project female bodies as equivalent to property (from historical plantation and indentured labor schemes) and are compounded by anxiety surrounding the control of women's sexuality (Trotz, 2003, p.17). Thus, this snapshot into Guyana's complex web of cultural dynamics, history, and social systems indicates the necessity for working practitioners to practice gender sensitivity and be aware of their own positionality when immersed in these environments.

Guyanese Demographics

Guyana, independent since 1966, is the only English-speaking country in South America and the two largest ethnic groups, Afro-Guyanese and the Indo-Guyanese, together comprise about three quarters of the country's population.

This ethnic diversity is reflected in the country's religious diversity as well: the two largest are Protestant 30.5%, (including Pentecostal, Anglican, Seventh Day Adventist, and Methodist), and Hindu 28.4%. The rest are primarily Roman Catholic, Muslim, and other smaller Christian groups.

About one-third of the Guyanese population lives below the poverty line; Indigenous people are disproportionately affected. Guyana's emigration rate is among the highest in the world - more than 55% of its citizens reside abroad - the pervasive emigration of skilled workers deprives Guyana of professionals in healthcare and other key sectors. (World Fact Book, 2013).

Several reports acknowledge that addressing violence and trauma is a significant need, not only in Guyana, but in many other countries as well. Especially critical for Guyana are the areas of suicide and violence. Guyana ranks #1 in death rate per 100,000 by suicide and in terms of violence within the country, Guyana ranks 29th per 100,000. (World Life Expectancy, 2014). Understanding the client's cultural views about suicide and violence is critical prior to planning an intervention.

Culturally Responsive Professional Action

This brief anthropological and demographic perspective on the culture of Guyana points to the importance of a practitioner needing to appreciate their own and their clients' cultural context, including mental health issues and possible interventions. Given the rich ethnic diversity of Guyana it is highly likely that practitioners may be of a different ethnic and religious group than their clients. Gender attitudes, family practices, and relationships with social services agencies could vary greatly between these groups, based on differences between urban and rural experiences. The religious diversity suggests that an understanding of the religious values of one's client is essential for placing their beliefs and practices within the context of the issues and challenges they face. Specific knowledge about the Amerindian communities, as well, is critical to serving that community well.

In any given culture how trauma is experienced, understood, and responded to will in some way determine what is even considered trauma. In an effort to provide culturally relevant services that are helpful to clients it is critically important to have an understanding of the cultural nuances and meaning attributed to events that are labeled as trauma.

While the cultural differences in Guyana are unique to its history and specific populations, every country has a range of economic, cultural, and social challenges that can lead to domestic violence, truancy, sexual assault, and schooling challenges around bullying, school attendance, and academic success. These issues occur across all populations, regardless of ethnic, social, economic, religious or cultural group, although in general, women and poor families are disproportionately affected.

In summary, in order for human services professionals to respond in culturally responsive ways to the variety of cultural contexts within Guyana, or any diverse community or nation, they must:

- Have a sociocultural consciousness
- Affirm views of clients from diverse backgrounds
- Be familiar with their own individual and family knowledge and beliefs
- Design interventions that build on what clients know and clients' lived experiences.

Cultural Humility: Openness to Others

The concept of Cultural Humility is valuable as a guide for affirming those from diverse backgrounds. Given the cultural complexity of Guyana, it is useful to build a quality of cultural humility, understanding cultural responsiveness as a process rather than an end product. (Waters and Asbill, 2014). From this perspective, competency involves more than gaining factual knowledge — it also includes our ongoing attitudes toward both our clients and ourselves. (Jones & Bullock, 2012)

Cultural humility is a construct for understanding and developing a process-oriented approach to cultural interaction. Hook, Davis, Owen, Worthington and Utsey (2013) conceptualize cultural humility as the "ability to maintain an interpersonal stance that is other-oriented (or open to the other) in relation to aspects of cultural identity that are most important to the [person]" (p. 2).

The first aspect of cultural humility is a lifelong commitment to self-evaluation and self-critique (Tervalon & Murray-Garcia, 1998). Because our knowledge is never finished, we approach what we know with humility and flexibility, engaging in self-reflection and a desire to learn more. We act on what we know, being open to adapting what we know, and building a greater understanding of those we serve.

The second feature of cultural humility is to acknowledge and challenge power imbalances (Tervalon & Murray-Garcia, 1998). We recognize the many power relationships within counseling, human services, and education that can determine the ways we use our individual power, and the power of our institutions. While a practitioner holds a body of knowledge that the client does not, the client also has understanding outside the scope of the practitioner, about his or her own life, personal history, and preferences.

Finally, cultural humility includes aspiring to develop partnerships with people and groups who advocate for others (Tervalon & Murray-Garcia, 1998). Though individuals can create positive change, communities and groups can also have a profound impact on systems. We cannot individually commit to self-evaluation and challenging power imbalances without advocating within the larger organizations in which we participate. Cultural humility, by definition, is larger than our individual selves — we must advocate for it systemically.

In our work as professionals and practitioners, we have a responsibility to recognize and value the diversity of our clients. We must enter our therapeutic and psycho-educational relationships with cultural humility, acknowledging that we are always in the process of learning and growing. (Waters, Asbill, 2014). Gallardo (2014) reminds us that while we approach this process with intention and seriousness, "we must not forget that engaging in cultural self-reflection and developing cultural humility are also personally liberating and gratifying." (p. 250).

Expressive Therapies Classroom, Lesley University

Cultural Insights and Personal Reflections

Given the need to provide effective community mental health services, psycho-educational workshops encourage participants and leadership to be open to new learning and engage together toward a shared goal. The Guyanese practitioners, in facilitating their workshops, found new insights about themselves, their clients and colleagues, and the issues they care deeply about. Learning can be transforming if one reflects on experiences, asking what happened and why, looking critically and fully at the interactions, workshop structure, and the cultural dynamics of those attending. While knowledge of cultural factors is required, it isn't always easy to take that knowledge and respond in an adept way. Practitioners need to approach this process of reflection with humility and an attitude of life-long learning.

The experiences of the professionals in the Lesley University/Guyana degree program highlight the variety of learning that is possible from this reflective, on-going process. Their statements, provided below, fall into several important cultural categories and insights.

*Without being aware of our own attitudes, and critically reflecting and looking deeply at these, our own prejudices may get in the way:

I am not fully multi-culturally competent but close to being there because of some basic values and beliefs that are embedded in me, not from my professional life alone. Mutual respect is the foundation for me in relation to multicultural competence, respecting others' customs, culture, and values that may be different from mine. I still need to grow in understanding power and oppression based on age, race, gender, religion, and class. (Hilliman)

Much of my job is conducted in the field, so I am constantly visiting communities and homes, acquiring a firsthand experience of the level of poverty that adolescents experience, especially in this region, including Amerindian and Afro-Guyanese. It is therefore very important to be culturally oriented when working in these communities. An in-depth understanding is required as it relates to the beliefs, religion, and practices of these different populations. It can be very easy to experience resistance from a population if one is not culturally oriented. (Hamandeo)

There are perceptions, stereotypes, that Afro-Guyanese youths or black youths in general are more prone to delinquency, and that Indo-Guyanese parents and adolescents do not access available services in a way intended to benefit all. At the beginning of the workshop I took care not to make prejudicial statements. The emphasis was on creating an atmosphere where participants were comfortable and saw the benefit of being at the workshop, instead of focusing on what stereotypes and differences may be brought to the workshop. Presentations were tailored to ensure none of the participants felt judged and the success of this was evident in the group's interaction. Their candid contributions to discussion were made with a high degree of respect. There has definitely been a major shift in my views on culture and people since the course exercise of reflecting on the impact of culture on my own life. I strongly believe that it is beneficial to have an understanding of where the person is, at that particular time, rather that assume and cause discomfort or cause them to feel prejudiced or judged. One can learn a lot by observation. (Crawford)

*Workshop facilitators found the need to be sensitive about gender dynamics, and saw that assumptions about gender are connected to other identities, such as ethnicity and class:

Sometimes a person of one racial or ethnic identity or gender might be uncomfortable working with a service provider who is of a different group. I have experienced times, due to my ethnicity, I am assumed to be of a specific political orientation. We need to be professional and culturally sensitive to our clients and refer the person if they so desire. In the past, I was angry and hurt at this type of behavior, but it is possible that a woman who was battered might be uncomfortable relating to a male counselor and a referral might be the best option. (Sharma)

I remember visiting one of our Primary Schools and observed some parents waiting for the lunch bell to feed their five and six year old children. I had never seen this action displayed by an Afro-Guyanese, only the Indo-Guyanese, and realized Afro-Guyanese women are mostly employed, and wouldn't be able to bring lunch to their children, they are employed in the low paying or lengthy hours job sector. When working in such situations with women from the rural area, I would need to be careful. I need to express more empathy towards these families since they are living in a rural area, have little access to some institutions for development, and whose culture and socialization is different than mine. So I need to not get frustrated with a mother of seven and lament over the fact that she did not practice family planning but I need to help her access the service or goods which she is in dire need of. For the women in the capital city, I would expect that they have more access to information on family planning and because they do not have access to a farm or kitchen garden they are aware the only way for them to feed their children is by working outside their home.

I have a colleague who is very comfortable working with this rural population since he lived among similar communities most of his years. He acknowledges the lack of resources and the effects of this on the population. Often times he would express his frustration about some of the official policies that are not catering for the parents living below the poverty line. He would ask me, "How can I instruct this young man to be suspended from school until his poor mother gets monies to alter his tight pants." He can relate to our clients' powerlessness. (Cameron)

*Effectively welcoming cultural difference means acknowledging and understanding issues of power and privilege within the community, the school, the family, and the nation.

The population that I serve is primarily made up of school-aged children and adolescents within the public school system. I work with parents and teachers and sometimes I also work with religious leaders, community groups, other networking social service departments, and other groups. Within this population there is diversity in every aspect of the dimensions of cultural identity, although there are mainly two predominant groups that occupy the schools and communities that I work in: the Indo Guyanese and the Afro Guyanese.

Issues of power and privilege relate to social class and educational status within this population. It is a normative belief that persons belonging to high socioeconomic class are given opportunities and preference. Political affiliation plays a great part in determining those who are marginalized and who aren't, who feels oppressed and who is given privileges. If one has relatives in high political office and/ or being associated with the political party in governance leads others to assume that one has some right to privileges more than others. These are far reaching aspects that extend even to the counseling office and can have effects on the relationship between the counselor and the client. (Persaud)

★Issues of power arise as the practitioner interacts with participants or clients, based on assumptions and stereotypes within the audience, and within him/herself. The practitioner can be the recipient of cultural stereotyping from others:

Participants at the workshop were not comfortable with me "lecturing" to them, especially as a junior teacher. Most of the teachers were senior in position with more years of service than me. It is the perception of Afro-Guyanese teachers that the Indo-Guyanese teachers cannot deal with the Afro-Guyanese students in terms of discipline. Most of the Afro-Guyanese teachers believe that other religions are inferior to their Christian religion. They do not participate in other religious festivals in school. I feel victimized if I publicly show support to a political party that they do not support. Many would not buy or read the government newspaper because they believe that the government is an "Indo-Guyanese government" who do not like "the Afro-Guyanese." History has shown that an election in Guyana is heavily based on race and not on policies. Knowing and experiencing these things has caused me many times to take a careful stance in working across cultures. (Bactawar)

As I began my work with the student population of the secondary school, I quickly observed that many of them were afraid of me. At first this took me by surprise; however, I quickly realized that their fears were mainly because I was a welfare officer and a government employee. I further discovered that many of the students and even their parents were of the belief that I was a probation welfare officer and that I was at the school to take the undisciplined students to the juvenile facility. Similarly many were of the notion that I was a political activist of the ruling political party who was at the school to enforce the will of the government.

These negative perceptions of the students and their parents were mainly because most of them were supporters of the Opposition Party and also because many of them have had unfortunate dealings with the probation welfare department and even had loved ones placed before the court and incarcerated by probation welfare officers.

Therefore I quickly realized that there were aspects of my work that had to be shifted. In order to gain the students' and their parents' trust I needed to emphasize to them that I am a Schools Welfare Officer and also that my political affiliation would not affect my work with them. I determined to work with the students and their parents in a manner that would suggest to them that I wasn't a probation welfare officer and that I was politically unaffiliated.

The first thing I did was to change my dress code to casual wear rather than the usual tie and suit and then the second thing I did was rather than work from behind a desk in an enclosed room, I started carrying out most of my work within the classrooms of the students and on the school's playfield. And finally, I removed all items I had at the school such as pens, books, photos, and such that could have suggested to my clients a political affiliation. (Zahaur)

★When cultural background and differences are seen not as a problem, but as an additional resource, many powerful and effective services result.

Cultural differences can be at play when treatment is offered by social service agencies, as behavioral issues with children and adolescents are often seen as actions and thoughts that the individual can adjust by will or by force through the application of certain consequences. Often when the mental and physical wellbeing of an individual is extremely compromised, it is customary and a shared belief by many that spiritual forces are at play and are responsible for these human dysfunctions. Families often turn to religion for answers. This faith and belief that the diverse cultures embrace in their respective religions has affected positive psychological changes among many individuals, while interfering with possible treatments in others. So in my work, I strive not to dismiss or challenge the beliefs of clients and their families, instead in many cases I encourage and help guide individuals towards recuperation via their cultural and religious beliefs and values. (Persaud)

Within the population I serve, there are several strengths, such as people's team spirit, abilities, and entrepreneurial competencies. They place a high value on harmony and tend to be strong advocates for social change. When dealing with conflict situations, many will exercise more patience because they have recognized that conflicts are inevitable and are an active part of life. The entrepreneurial qualities allow them to maintain themselves and family members and actively provide food and employment. They take pride in their cultural beliefs and customs, displaying a variety of skills. This gives me hope. (Dyall)

The workshop participants arrived at the consensus that it was part of the general Guyanese culture regardless of any subculture that there is an extended family network, coupled with the multiplicity of faith-based organizations that as social workers we can tap into to assist with care and support for victims of domestic violence. (Sharma)

In conducting this workshop I was able to identify strengths, skills, and problem-solving abilities that may be available to the population in which I serve. Some of the strengths are that of resilience, a strong sense of religion and spirituality and common values across all cultures. I have been celebrating the cultural heritage of the members of my population and much emphasis is placed on their beliefs and values. In other words, they were treated with dignity and respect in regard to their culture, religion, or ethnicity. (Pearson)

A strength noted from the workshop was that participants were able to identify the social issues affecting each community from a multicultural viewpoint. The participants were very receptive to information presented which was noted in the continued discussion even during the short interval for snacks; thus I believe that it is important to utilize and create a stronger networking with participants, who I personally considered community activists for children against abuse, and information they share can be instrumental in the development of polices relating to children in their communities. (Gonsalves)

Reflective Questions for the Reader:

As a leader/presenter, what are your areas for self-reflection? What are the aspects of your cultural identity that are most important to you?

What are the attributes and dynamics of the population you serve that you might reflect on further?

Chapter II: Advocacy and Education: Strategy for Increasing Capacity

Practitioners who bring new skills, information, and techniques to a region or community must be equipped with not only the content of the material but also the skills involved in disseminating the content effectively to the particular audience.

This chapter outlines the basic processes involved in developing workshops, conference presentations, department meetings, and group sessions with parents, educators, and professional colleagues. These sessions often draw upon concepts from counseling and an understanding of trauma. It is important to stress again that this is not counseling or therapy. Rather these are psycho-educational workshops that have a learning goal for the participants. As such there is an educational focus and somewhat different guidelines than in a counseling context.

Academic Frameworks

1. People learn best by doing, engaging, and connecting material to experience, rather than by listening to someone telling them information.
2. Participants (students, clients, colleagues) have knowledge (lived experiences) that leads to concepts and creative solutions. It is important to listen to people's stories.
3. Art and expressive activities can be important components of psycho-educational practice.
4. Critical reflection about experiences is a significant aspect of learning.

Experiential Learning

1. *Effective Learning*

Adults learn most effectively when they can be fully engaged in the learning process. Adults need to know why they should learn something, rather than simply listen to presented information. The purpose of the information and the value to the learner needs to be clearly stated. Adults also learn best when they can be self-directing, taking an active role in their own learning process.

Adults have a wide range of life experiences, and appreciate learning opportunities that draw on these experiences. While they may not know the theory about a topic, they often have specific experiences that they can relate to the topic at hand. Adults tend to enter a learning experience with a problem-solving or life-centered orientation. Presentations that focus material through problems or experience and offer participants a way to take part in the process are often the most successful. One facilitator found this set of parameters especially useful:

Our discussion was interactive as all the participants were practitioners and court officers drawn from the probation department. Therefore, personalized first hand observation and experiences were shared. The real-life examples reinforced an interest as we all shared our concerns and built support systems between us to act in a unified manner. (Sharma)

2. *People's Stories*

Each person has a story to tell, a lived experience, which can offer rich texture to discussion, or help the practitioner understand a seemingly confusing or troubling situation, as in this story:

> One of my key functions as a Senior Schools Welfare Officer is to address attendance and punctuality in schools. Through my investigations on the job I learned that in a certain riverine Amerindian area attendance in schools on Mondays is less that 4.0%. This area has 15 schools so this was an alarming concern for my department. When I went into the area, parents told me that Monday is market day for that area and the whole family would go to market. When I inquired about when this pattern had begun, the parents related that since they were kids their parents took them on Mondays to market so they are doing the same with their kids. Normally I would create a system to charge parents for neglecting to send their children to school but after understanding that this is a cultural issue, I changed my approach and initiated a series of meetings held in the communities to sensitize parents about the importance of an education for their children. (Hamandeo)

3. *Accessing the Arts*

The use of arts-based interventions in psycho-educational workshops can provide a powerful means to engage clients and have inherent therapeutic value as well. In the following example, meaningful movement exercise enhanced workshop participants' understanding of domestic violence:

> Participants were asked to stand in a straight line having one person controlling at the front acting as the abuser (father/spouse), giving hand directions to the second person as the victim (mother), who has to follow the directions and pass on directions to the other member and the third person as the affected child and it follows to the bottom to other family members, peers, community members and other social networks. Participants shared their views on this aspect of the activity and they all recognize how difficult it was to be receiving a forceful direction and how it was passed on unconsciously to the followers. (Ramphal)

Similarly, mindfulness practices added to workshops and programs serve to deepen participant attention and engagement as well as offer a therapeutic benefit.

> I conducted a five-minute body scan to relax participants and promote self-care. Some of the participants attended the workshop after a hectic day of work. (Gonsalves)

> After returning for the second session of the workshop, I asked the participants to sit in their seats, close their eyes and do a deep breathing exercise. My goal for letting them partake in this exercise was to get them relaxed and focused for the next session. (Zahaur)

4. *Critical Reflection*

An attitude of critical reflection leads to meaningful learning. Such reflection considers the context of an event or experience, especially issues of power and culture. In fact, the most effective workshops are often those where participants and facilitator are open to new learning and engaging together toward a shared goal. Deep, personal and power-aware reflection led to many new insights for the educators and human service professionals in the Guyana Program. Insights about themselves, their clients, and the context in which they work provided deeper understanding of the needs of participants, relevant content, and facilitation strategies.

Learning can be transforming when one reflects on experiences, asking what happened and why, looking critically and fully at the interactions, workshop structure, and the cultural dynamics of those attending. In addition, the attitude and skills of the facilitators are always developing. While knowledge of cultural factors is required, it isn't always easy to use that knowledge to respond in an adept way. Facilitators need to approach this process of reflection with humility and an attitude of life-long learning. This was an important facet of one practitioner's reflection about her workshop:

> The fact that five parents who were selected to attend the workshop and who are all of East Indian ethnicity did not show up was certainly food for thought for me. Maybe I was being prejudicial, stereotypical or biased, but to my mind, it confirmed that this group of parents was not interested in their children's schooling, since they were not participating in an activity that would have benefitted them as parents and ultimately their children.
>
> I sought answers to ascertain whether my opinions were true and found that I was being prejudicial. I learned that one of those five parents was unable to

attend the workshop because she was unable to leave her business since she couldn't find someone to take over in her absence. Since she couldn't attend the workshop, the other four parents decided that they would not attend the workshop either.

Reflecting further, looking deeper, and talking with colleagues, I also learned that the participants of the East Indian ethnic group may not have attended the workshop because they felt as though there was no one that they could have connected with, especially since as facilitator, I am of African descent.

I learned that having a co-facilitator who is of East Indian descent could create that ethnic identity and compatibility for the participants who are East Indian. And as such, they may be more willing to attend other workshops and participate fully. (Pearson)

Workshop/Event Design Components

The design of the workshops builds on the Academic Frameworks, supporting the effective ways adults learn. Psycho-educational workshops include the components listed below; explanations and examples follow the chart. Further examples are found within the specific workshop descriptions in the next chapter.

Workshop Design Components

1. Pre-workshop Preparation:
   Goals, Objectives, Content, Materials, Logistics
2. Opening:
   Welcoming, stating goals, sharing the agenda,
   establishing ground rules and a safe environment
3. Presenting content in an interactive format:
   Short talks, power points, videos, charts, case
   studies, role-play, small and large group discussion,
   expressive arts, self-care activities
4. Closing:
   Next steps, appreciations, and evaluation

1. Pre-Workshop Preparation

Workshops begin by determining the goals and objectives of the workshop and identifying the characteristics of the appropriate participants. For example, participants could be colleagues within a department, agency, or school, or parents, caregivers, or community members. Determining the content for the workshop depends on the context or situation, the learning goals, and the needs and interests of the workshop participants.

There are several ways to clarify these goals and needs, which will insure that the topic and the general goals of the workshop serve those who attend. Contacting potential participants to assess needs and interest can be done in several ways: by sending out questionnaires, meeting with potential participants as you plan, or presenting plans at meetings with colleagues prior to the presentation.

Examples:
   I had researched the targeted community preceding
   the workshop in order to be better equipped with
   additional information that the participants needed
   to understand about the community and the social issue
   of the workshop from a micro, mezzo and macro level.

Additionally, the participants had interacted with me at other forums or at the professional level in the past, resulting in the selection to participate. (Gonsalves)

The needs assessment and interviews that were conducted to help ascertain what knowledge and skills teachers were in need of in order to help combat physical violence at the school was extremely effective in that they clearly decided on the workshop focus. Teacher's involvement in selecting an area of focus for the workshop was one of the factors that made the new group of teachers in actual attendance as welcoming and receptive of the workshop as they were. Teachers expressed a sense of partnership, especially since the content of the workshop was not imposed upon them, but resonated greatly with their own needs. (Persaud)

2. Opening, Welcoming, Agenda, Introductions

The opening moments set the tone for the workshop. Adults want to know why they are there and what is important for them about the workshop. They also want to know who is there, and feel comfortable that the facilitator is going to acknowledge and honor what they bring with them about the topic. Adults want to be in a space where they feel safe to offer their ideas and know the rules of participation. This sense of safety can be achieved by opening exercises that make participants feel comfortable, sharing the agenda, and by making ground rules explicit. Adults also want to share authority for what happens in the group, and the arrangement of chairs within the room in a semicircle or U shape says the participants are part of the process and have authority along with the facilitator.

We opened with an opening circle- 'getting to know you'. Participants described something about themselves by giving a name of a fruit they would like to be if they had the choice. This exercise was fun and exciting and we used a soft toy and a ball to identify the next person for the activity. The participants were open-minded; they quickly bought into the idea and loosened up for the remainder of the workshop. (Jardine)

The activity 'What's in my name' was used as a means to get participants to know each other, help them to be present and focused on what was taking place in the space. It also allowed them to explore their feelings about something that was placed upon them without their involvement or input: their names. Each participant was asked to say their name and tell the group something that stands out to them about their name, whether positive or not. This activity was well received by the participants and saw total involvement. It set the stage for smooth transition into the first subject for discussion. (Sharma)

Ground Rules/Safe Space:

I encouraged participants before the commencement of the workshop presentation to establish ground rules collectively which they felt would be of importance for the group. This resulted in the participants agreeing that no over talking was permitted when another participant was sharing. I felt that participants needed to be reassured that the information shared or disclosed during discussions would be kept in confidentiality by the group in order for participants to be more open and comfortable with sharing their views of the topic being presented, therefore I added confidentially to the ground rules, and the group agreed. (Gonsalves)

3. Interactive Formats for Presenting Content

The most effective workshops invite participants into the learning process. This can be done in many ways: small group discussion, role-playing, brainstorming, large group discussion, expressive arts activities, and visual presentations, to list a few.

Power Point, Handouts, Follow-up Discussion

> After the power point presentations were concluded the group was then divided into mini groups for discussion and presentations. Because I wanted the participants to interact with each other from different schools and communities, I requested that each group have teachers, parents and stakeholders from different locations in the region. Given questions to discuss and create recommendations, the groups were in discussion for thirty minutes after which two groups presented before lunch. (Hamandeo)

> Participants were placed into three groups after the PowerPoint presentation to elicit discussion, based on several questions provided on a handout. Each group received a different question to answer. Subsequently each group presented their information while the other groups made comments and recommendations. (Bactawar)

Videos

> I set the stage for my workshop by showing the three and a half minute music video "Don't Laugh at Me". The song was written by Allen Shamblin and Steve Seskin and it was originally recorded by the American country music artist Mark Wills. However because the participants at my workshop were Afro Guyanese who are very fond of Hip Hop music, I decided to use

the Hip Hop version of the song which was recorded by Baby Jay. While the song focused on asking for acceptance and respect from others, it also highlighted many scenarios and forms of violent student behaviors. (Zahaur)

Case Study:

Examples of situations or individuals that connect to the content of the workshop, followed by discussion questions in small groups, inviting participants to analyze and suggest responses, depending on the presenter's goals.

> A short case study was read as an example of one child's experience and responses when parents divorced. We followed with discussion of ways to provide support to the child and the parents. (Dyall)

Clay as an Expressive Medium

Expressive/Experiential Activity

Participants are given a paper that had a circle divided in two. The top half of the circle asked them to write "how they think others see them" and at the bottom half of the circle, they were asked to write "how they feel inside." After the completion of this activity participants were asked to share their responses, which generated lively discussion. This session was extremely interactive and the parents were fully involved and vocal. This activity was selected because it gave the parents an opportunity to introspect, they were able to express the way they truly feel, as well as identify some of the internal struggles they were experiencing. (Pearson)

The Human Knot is an experiential activity that enables participants to understand how difficult it might be for a young person or a parent to get out of a situation, but once help is sought through networking it would be easier for them to respond.

Participants were divided into two groups of eight persons, each group was asked to form a circle facing inward, then participants were asked to reach into the center of the circle and firmly clasp hands or wrists with 2 different people Without letting go, participants were then asked to work together and try to untangle themselves from the knot and then reform the circle.

After the exercise participants shared their views of the activity. One of the main things mentioned was the difficulty experienced to untie the knot. At this point participants were asked to visualize how difficult it is for a child who is tied up in multiple issues, such as poverty, single parent home, separation of parent, death of loved ones, learning problems, and teacher issues to untie themselves from such. (Hilliman)

<u>*Energizer/Transitions*</u>

When the group has a break for lunch, or has been involved in one activity for a long time, participants may need an energizer or way to refocus their attention to the workshop activity. There are many ways to do this, with physical activity or mindful, focused activity.

> After returning for the second session of the workshop, I asked the participants to sit in their seats, close their eyes and do a deep breathing exercise. My goal for letting them partake in this exercise was to get them relaxed and focused for the next session. (Zahaur)

> The participants stood in a circle, threw a make-believe "energy ball" across the circle to another participant, who said his or her own name. This continued until each person had a chance to throw the "ball" and receive it.

> In order to quiet and focus attention, participants were engaged in a "Mind chatter" exercise. First, participants spent about 3 minutes to write down any mind chatter they were experiencing at that moment. If it included anything they must do, they would write it at the top of the page. If it were "nuisance" chatter, they would write it at the bottom of the page. When it was complete, they tore the top ("must do") from the bottom ("nuisance"). Then they gleefully threw the papers in the trash bin. (Persaud)

4. Closing and Evaluations/Feedback

It is important to end the workshop or meeting at the scheduled time. Instead of going right up to the final moment with the content or allowing discussion to go over, build time within the agenda to bring the workshop to a formal end. The closing is a time to summarize main points and/or recommendations determined by the group. It may include participants setting intentions for their own or their agency or school's next steps. This is a time for participants to speak about their experience and offer appreciations.

Participant Feedback

The closing offers an opportunity to collect feedback from participants. A feedback form for group members encourages them to say what they found helpful, what suggestions they have, and any other specific information the facilitator wants to collect. The forms may have questions, with room for participants to write their answers. The information may be arranged in a Likert Scale, giving participants a chance to rate their experience. You may wish to use oral or visual responses, such as taping a feedback discussion, or using a page with faces of various expressions to give the feedback. The questions can be read aloud, if there is a reading or language barrier. The facilitator could also invite smaller groups of 2 or 3 to discuss the questions and have one person write or report their responses.

Examples:
>   At the end of the workshop the same questionnaires were reapplied to participants as they had filled out at the beginning of the workshop and the totality showed great improvements in their responses. It was evident that teachers and parents that participated in the workshop were more equipped with knowledge in helping children affected by domestic violence. (Ramphal)

During the workshop, on-going observation as participants reflected on their experiences and practiced the ideas during discussion and activities allowed me to assess their understanding of the material, and also gave me ideas of how to continue to make the discussion relevant. At the end I passed out a sheet with four questions, with room for participants to write answers: What are three things you found most helpful in this workshop? What are three things that would make this workshop more effective? What suggestions do you have for future workshops? Any other comments? I received important feedback—both positive and useful critique. (Cameron)

Facilitator Self-Evaluation

Facilitators also need to do their own assessment of the learning or effectiveness of their workshop. Personal reflection, often with a colleague, can be important in order to continually build and improve future workshops. The facilitator can ask several questions in evaluating the workshop effectiveness.

Did the workshop give participants the chance to reflect on their own experience?

Did it provide ways of assimilating and conceptualizing new information? This usually involves theories, data, and facts. Presentation mode could be short lecture, case study, power point, or other media.

Did participants experiment and practice? Practice encourages application of the new knowledge learned and involvement in new behaviors and skills.

Assessing workshop challenges leads to stronger future experiences.

Examples:

The first thing that affected the workshop was the unavailability of a projector. My intention was to use a PowerPoint presentation that would facilitate the learning with colorful and visual aids that would stimulate great interaction. It would also benefit persons with different cognitive or learning styles. Consequently the presentation was presented in a slower manner. Even with this projector challenge, the session was very interactive. I try not being a teacher that wants to look superior to the participants so I ensure participants share when comfortable. I myself also shared with participants. During the presentation I used the term 'we' often implying that we are all in it together and not single out myself. Participants expressed thanks for the information and appeared eager for more in relation to the topic. (Hilliman)

For future workshops special attention would be given to the participants' literacy level. While participants were able to comprehend the information shared and be actively involved in discussions, some of them were unable to complete the evaluation sheet. An assessment of this kind should be the honest feedback of someone anonymous. Other evaluation feedback techniques will be explored for future workshops. (Crawford)

Sample Agendas

Workshops, conferences, and staff meetings can vary in length, from an hour or two to a full day. Other variables include the setting, number of participants, and ways of designing the agenda, based on the academic framework and workshop components. Here are samples of a full-day experience and a shorter workshop, to provide one template for how your event may be organized.

1. Full-Day Workshop/Event

Agenda:

9:00	Participants arrive, receive agenda, pen/paper, coffee available
9:15	Opening Welcome and Statement about Workshop Goals, Agenda
9:30	Introductions and Establishing Ground Rules
10:00	Interactive Content/Presentation/Discussion
10:20	Break
10:50	Brainstorm, small group discussion, group summaries on large sheets of paper
11:15	Large group discussion
11:45	Lunch. Participants bring lunch. Coffee and sweets provided.
12:30	Return from lunch, energizer/transition activity, and short discussion.
12:45	Content/presentation
1:10	Experiential Activity: Personal Reflection
1:45	Discussion/Professional Application
2:10	Evaluations and Closing
2:30	End of Workshop

2. Half-day Workshop/Event

Agenda	
1:00	Participants arrive, receive agenda, pen/paper, coffee, snack.
1:10	Welcome and Statement of Goals for the afternoon
1:15	Introductions, Creating a Safe Space/Ground rules, Share Agenda
1:40	Interactive Content/presentation
2:10	Discussion groups
2:30	Role Play and Reflections
3:30	Closing and Evaluations
4:00	End of Workshop

Note: Even with a half-day workshop, it is important to spend time with the welcome and closing, as well as include active experiential learning.

Chapter III: Sample Workshops Promoting Community Mental Health

This chapter summarizes each of the workshops completed by the graduates of the Lesley University/Guyana Degree Program, including goals, content summary, and special features. The workshops fell into three broad categories: Family Dynamics, Schools and Educational Settings, and Communities.

Workshops Related to Family Dynamics

Several workshops focused on the ways in which parents can support their children and professionals can support parents.

Parental Involvement in Interventions with Youths/Adolescents in Contact With the Law

Facilitator: Oslyn L. Crawford

Goal: The workshop focused on developing skills for parental involvement with youths/adolescents already in contact with the law. Participants included parents or guardians of youths connected to Probation, Voluntary Supervision, or Community Service. The half-day workshop was designed for 25 participants.

Content: included influences on adolescents/youth behavior, the ecological and the psychosocial models of development, and the role of parents or guardians/caregivers during this period of transition from childhood into adulthood. Discussion emphasized strategies resulting in targeted interventions.

Special Features: materials to take home, awareness of literacy in developing evaluations.

Care was taken so that the information presented to parents was clear and could be easily understood. Parents could take home reading materials as points of reference, including two diagrams explaining the ecological model presented, and the stages of growth and development.

For future workshops special attention would be given to the participants' literacy level. While participants were able to comprehend the information shared and be actively involved in discussions, some of them were unable to complete the evaluation sheet. Though the views expressed during discussions were similar to those conveyed on the assessment sheet, an assessment of this kind should be the honest feedback of someone anonymous. Other evaluation feedback techniques will be explored for future workshops.

Divorce –A Critical Social Problem Tearing Families and Guyana Apart
Facilitator: Sharon Dyall
Goal: An analysis of challenges faced by adolescent children of divorced parents led to the goal to promote the family systematic approach in intervention to bring about positive behavioral changes by the children. The one-day workshop was divided into two segments, meeting with children in the morning and parents in the afternoon.

Content: Introduced multiple emotional and behavioral challenges for many children whose parents have divorced, such as poor social and communication skills, poor academic achievement, domestic violence and family conflict, mental health issues, adjustment issues, and resulting trauma. The presentation included strategies for parents to decrease the traumatic impacts of divorce.

Special Features: guest speaker, introductions and welcome. The supervisor of an office or region may welcome the participants, or reflect on the presentation and add his/her voice to the discussion.

Since one goal was for participants to approach workshop activities in a relaxed manner, they sat in a circle and were asked to share aloud a word to describe how they felt about being at this workshop. The aim of this activity was to build strong interpersonal bonds and the ability to be comfortable with each other.

Parenting Made Fun: Promoting Positive Parent/Child Relationships
Facilitator: Onika Pearson
Goal: Help parents recognize positive parental supervision and support at home that could support children and adolescents to perform better academically and exhibit less delinquent behaviour. The workshop developed parenting skills and knowledge needed to support and motivate children academically. Twenty parents who are part of the PTA body of the schools their children attend were invited, selected from four communities, for the half-day workshop.

Content: Positive parenting skills, social learning theory, the benefits of home school collaboration, and time management tips. The group developed recommendations for future support.

Special Features: combining creative expression, welcome, and evaluation
The workshop began with an invitation to participants to take a sheet that showed faces with different emotions, and circle the face that best matched their emotion in beginning the workshop. The close for the workshop was a time to have reflections on the day's activity where persons briefly shared their thoughts. After this the participants were given an evaluation sheet to share their opinion regarding the sessions and activities. The participants were also asked to refer to the paper with the different images of emotions and were asked to circle the face that expressed the emotion they were feeling now that the workshop was coming to an end. There was a brief discussion regarding the responses. All the participants mentioned that they had positive changes in their emotions.

Posters completed by Children

Workshops Related to Schools and Educational Settings.

Several of the program graduates focused their thesis workshop studies on implications of violence, domestic insecurity, and poverty on students' academic success.

Social Factors that Contribute to the Academic Achievement of Students in Rural Communities in Guyana
Facilitator: Stephen Bactawar
Goal: The workshop brought teachers at a regional school together for a half-day workshop seeking deeper insight into factors leading to students' poor academic performance, and the implications for both parents and teachers.

Content: Identifying factors contributing to academic performance and focus on ways teachers can support parents to read to their children, help children finish school assignments, provide a quiet place for study and doing assignments, and motivate and encourage children with positive words and rewards.

Special Features: documentation/data, small groups, recommendation/ time.

Data included charts of Caribbean Secondary School Examination results and National Grade Nine Examination results, highlighted to show student performance over time.

Participants were placed into three groups after the PowerPoint presentation to elicit discussion, based on several questions provided on a handout. Each group received a different question to answer. Subsequently each group presented their information while the other groups made comments and recommendations.

I observed that using the school's time to conduct a workshop was not the best thing to do because many classes were out of teachers, thus leaving the students unsupervised. A week- end workshop would be more comfortable and productive. More teachers would be able to participate rather than the few who were selected for the workshop. Also, the environment would be more conducive, rather than hearing the school's bell and noise from the children.

Coping With Poverty To Improve Academic Performance
Facilitator: Haimraj Hamandeo
Goal: Focus on poverty and its impact on academic performances in secondary schools and ways in which we can help adolescents in the classroom deal with the stressors of being poor, in order to improve their academic performance. The full day workshop included 32 teachers, parents, and community stakeholders.

Content: Summary of research conducted around the topic; the need for teachers to create an environment and social climate that embodies respect towards adolescents in poverty; ways to make students part of decision making in the classrooms, and strategies that embed social skills for students so they can strengthen their social and emotional ability and improve their academic performance.

Special Features: mindfulness activity, power point and group discussion.
A mindful breathing exercise was done to begin the day's proceedings. This exercise lasted for about 10 minutes. This was a wonderful experience, not only for me but also for the participants because for

the first time they were able to experience such an activity. At first they were not so much into the activity and found it to be a little funny, but after a couple of minutes I observed that they were starting to indulge completely into the activity. I conducted this activity because I wanted the participants to experience something new and fascinating that would help them relax and open up their minds for the day's activities.

After the power point presentations were concluded the group was then divided into mini groups for discussion and presentations. Because I wanted the participants to interact with each other from different schools and communities, I requested that each group have teachers, parents and stakeholders from different locations in the region. Given questions to discuss and create recommendations, the groups were in discussion for thirty minutes after which two groups presented before lunch.

Early Indicators of Truancy and Intervention Strategies
Facilitator: Lotoya Hilliman
Goal: Work with truant students led to her goal to explore information about truancy, in order to decrease the incidence of truant behavior. Ten professionals who work with high-risk children, in and out of school, attended the half-day workshop.

Content: Identify early indicators of trauma and discussion led to developing intervention strategies for combating the issue.

Special Features: pre and post assessment activity, welcoming adults. For the purpose of evaluation, a pre assessment and post assessment were conducted. The pre-assessment was a questionnaire prior to the workshop, given to probable participants, to gather information on their knowledge of the topic. That assessment revealed that appropriate and workable intervention was a major challenge faced by professionals working with these children. The post assessment was achieved as part of the final evaluation form.

I try not being a teacher that wants to look superior to the participants so I ensure participants share when comfortable. I myself also shared with participants. During the presentation I used the term 'we' often implying that we are all in it together and not single out myself. Participants expressed thanks for the information and appeared eager for more in relation to the topic.

Physical Violence Among Children in School: Elaborating a Mechanism to Tackle Physical Violence
Facilitator: Sewpaul Persaud
Goal: Decrease physical violence among students of grade nine classrooms by expanding teachers' knowledge of and skill in providing conflict resolution. Ninth-grade teachers from one school spent a full day of a proposed three-part series.

Content: Predictors of youth violence among high school adolescents, teacher's responsibilities in terms of preventing violence among school children, and types, frequency, and dynamics of these incidents. Also an introduction of mechanisms useful in deterring physical violence in school, especially conflict resolution practices.

Special Features: pre-workshop planning, dividing into groups. Information from a randomly selected focus group of 13 teachers helped determine the knowledge and skills that teachers need to help address the issue of physical violence. Findings from the initial needs assessment strongly indicated that teachers wanted knowledge and skills in conflict resolution to help decrease and further prevent physical violence among students in the school.

Two ways to break into smaller groups - Participants "untangle the string to find out who were their partners. Participants share their responses with their partner, given 5 minutes each, and then determine what information they will bring back to the full group. Another time, I divided the participants into small groups, using matching cards from a deck of playing cards to do this.

The Effects of Domestic Violence on Children's Academic Performance and School Attendance

Facilitator: Vickchand Ramphal

Goal: Improve the academic performance and attendance of children in the schools across one region by creating awareness among teachers and parents on the effects of domestic violence on children's academic performance and attendance in school. Eighteen teachers and parents from one region attended the full day workshop.

Content: Definition of domestic violence, types of domestic violence, effects of domestic violence on children and their academic performance and attendance in school, the ecological systems model of behavior, and how teachers can play an important role in helping children that are affected by domestic violence.

Special Features: experiential presentation, evaluation, and mindfulness activity.

Participants were asked to arrange themselves in pairs, facing each other. One person was deemed the controller (abuser) standing with his/her hand placed in front of the face of the other person. The second person moved his/her head and body in the direction of the hand of the controller. Then after a few moments, they interchanged positions and did the same action. Participants shared their views and all of them said that they did not like the part where they were controlled by the movements of another person but they enjoyed being the person controlling. This led to a stimulating discussion.

As part of the opening, participants were invited to sit in a relaxed position and a tape was played to support participants in mindful relaxing, which the group experienced for 10 minutes.

Pre and post workshop questionnaires were used to collect data in the following areas: knowledge participants had on the topic, the ways forward for future workshops, and the general evaluation of the workshop."

Fostering of Empathy Within Classrooms as a Means of Combating Physical Bullying

Facilitator: Azharuddin Ahmad Rahat Zahaur

Goal: Support teachers in building empathy in their classroom as a strategy to combat bullying. Teachers from one school building met for a half-day session.

Content: Defining and identifying bullying, what steps can be taken to prevent its occurrences and ways to foster empathy within their classrooms as a strategy for decreasing the occurrence of bullying.

Special Features: role play, introductions, active sharing of group reports.

I gave each group a handout describing a classroom or schoolyard incident. In groups of 5, the participants were asked to take 10 minutes to plan role play scenarios. After the 10 minutes was up each group then role played their scenarios. Another handout held discussion questions to analyze, followed by group discussion of insights, surprises, and reactions, as well as implications for their school. I choose a role playing exercise because most of the teachers of the school are very fond of acting and drama and also because I believe by acting out these scenarios they would be able to better understand the situations.

Because our topic can be such a sensitive one and people are more comfortable talking to each other when they have established some relationship, it is best to use an ice breaker to begin. The activity which I used was for the group to walk around in a circle and each participant says their names in any tones they want while the rest of the group mimics it."

Workshops Focusing on Communities

Many of the problems of violence and trauma are community-wide, and take a comprehensive approach in reaching solutions. This includes attitudes toward mental health, domestic violence, and sexual abuse.

<u>Social Action through the Lens of Mental Health: Understanding and Maintaining Good Mental Health.</u>
Facilitator: Juanita Cameron
Goal: Reflect on current perceptions of mental health, given the traditional culture, in which mental illness is often connected to stigma and discrimination. Ten participants, a mix of parents, teachers, and staff colleagues attended the half-day workshop.

Content: Defining "mental health," acknowledging our Guyanese cultural assumptions, and encouraging care based on mental health concepts.

Special Features: video, handouts.
I chose a motivational presentation on reducing stigma and discrimination against mental illness. The presenter had her PhD in Psychology, is Canadian born while her parents originated from Barbados. The presenter shares many commonalities with the workshop participants: African background, Muslim, parents from the Caribbean, and speaking of one of the very problems we are faced with in Guyana. By learning that a country so close to ours was affected by mental health problems and were taking similar steps to address same would encourage the participants to receive and utilize the knowledge.

The use of the Power Point software to present the information was quite refreshing and allowed for participants to remain focused. The use of diagrams within the presentation also enforced the effectiveness of the delivery of the information. Receiving handouts to take away with the content and even a copy of the presentation (as requested) was effective since participants are armed with the information.

The Risk Factors Associated with Child Sexual Abuse Among Females in Charity/Pomeroon

Facilitator: Priscilla Gonsalves

Goal: Define risk factors associated with child sexual abuse and identify coordinated ways for the community to address the issue. The full-day workshop invited professional and non-professional individuals who interact with the targeted community on a daily basis.

Content: Presentation of research about risk factors, clarifying definitions and legal responsibilities of caregivers, recommendations for preventative methods that can be implemented into service delivery, and development of new polices to reduce child sexual abuse from occurring in the targeted communities.

Special features: setting safe space, community-wide participation.
I encouraged participants before the commencement of the workshop presentation to establish ground rules collectively which they felt would be of importance for the group. This resulted in the participants agreeing that no over talking was permitted when another participant was sharing. I felt that participants needed to be reassured that the information shared or disclosed during discussions would be kept in confidentiality by the group in order for participants to be more open and comfortable with sharing their views of the topic being presented, therefore I added confidentially to the ground rules, and the group agreed.

After the introductory power point with definitions, a short case study was read and discussed with the participants as an example of how sexual abuse may affect the child psychologically. Participants were able to identify with the discussion as a few of them had experienced similar situations in a residential facility and others mentioned other instances of abuse.

A Guide For Caregivers To Provide Adequate Care to Sexually Abused Children
Facilitator: Kaycina Jardine
Goal: Improve the lives of children residing in residential care facilities. Care providers and volunteers were invited for the one-day session.

Content: Signs, symptoms and impact of sexual abuse, trauma assessment, assessment tools, and further strategies to care for and protect children's welfare. Focus also on Self-care for participants.
Special Features: opening, self-care, special speakers, power point presentation.
We opened with an opening circle- 'getting to know you'. Participants described something about themselves by giving a name of a fruit they would like to be if they had the choice. This exercise was fun and exciting and we used a soft toy ball to identify the next person for the activity. The participants were open-minded; they quickly bought into the idea and loosened up for the remainder of the workshop.

I practice self-care/mindfulness practice for myself, as I offer this model for caregivers. I sit and focus my breath on my present state, whatever it is at the moment. It does not have to be for exactly twenty minutes. It can be for ten or even five minutes. The important thing is when my mind wonders, I notice that and return to focusing on my breath…. I found this to be very relaxing.

Aftercare for Victims of Domestic Violence: Emphasizing Psychological Trauma
Facilitator: Anand Sharma
Goal: Explore the issue of aftercare for victims of domestic violence, identify gaps in the services provided to persons who were abused and still have issues of depression and trauma, and strategize recommendations for action. Ten probation officers participated in the half-day workshop.

Content: Experiences of victims of domestic violence, where gaps in coverage occur, possible methods for providing aftercare, recommendations for staff training and providing consistent care.

Special Features: Setting safe space, mindfulness.

We agreed that certain ground rules would be respected such as one person who holds the bottle would stand and share his or her views without any crosstalk from the rest of the audience. This went very well as it was unanimously adopted. This also helped to bring the group together as colleagues and friends who supported each other and served to build mutual respect and appreciation for each other.

To get the participants in a calm, receptive state for our workshop after the overview we had a brief 5-minute session of mindfulness breathing. This set the tone for focus and attention to the topics of the day.

Chapter IV. Sustainability: Self Care for the Practitioner

Self-care serves an important function for practitioners, particularly for those who provide services to clients and communities experiencing trauma. In 1990 Pearlman and McCann coined the term "vicarious trauma" to describe the specific process by which psychotherapists who worked with survivors of trauma were impacted by the work. Over the last two decades the concept has expanded to include all practitioners who serve those who have been traumatized, including humanitarian workers, first responders, clergy, educators, and clinicians. The essence of the concept is that when we empathically engage with the one who suffers there is a process of transformation that concurrently occurs within the one who provides the service. The transformation, often similar to the symptoms experienced by the trauma survivor, is cumulative and the extent and nature determined by the practitioner's own personal history and context. A practitioner with a personal trauma history has particular vulnerabilities, especially when the trauma of their clients parallels their own personal narrative. Individuals who are new to the field as well as those with high caseloads and minimal support systems are also especially vulnerable. (Pearlman & Saakvitne, 1995).

Vicarious traumatization of the practitioner manifests in changes to many aspects of our self, including spirituality, physical and emotional well being, and cognitive functioning. In the face of profound suffering many practitioners find themselves struggling with spiritual questions such as —Where is God in the face of this cruelty and injustice? How do I make sense of this? Why did this happen? Many practitioners begin to have physical symptoms such as difficulty falling asleep and/or staying asleep, weight gain or loss, physical pains, being easily startled, or having nightmares. Emotional impact can include free floating anger and irritation, feelings of hopelessness and depression, inability to talk about feelings, sense of loss, worry, diminished joy, intense fear as well as feeling trapped particularly within one's work. Cognitive impact can include being distracted and inattentive, forgetful, or having intrusive thoughts. Interpersonally, one can begin to withdraw from previously supportive relationships and become isolated, or conversely one can become intensely needy and clingy or combative with colleagues and loved ones. (Pearlman & Saakvitne, 1995).

Braiding Raffia

There are many resources about vicarious trauma including online courses now available that practitioners are encouraged to explore. Links to these resources are provided below. The recommendations provided to our practitioners from Guyana that they found most helpful include the following:

1. Be aware of your vulnerability to the process of vicarious trauma and do not be ashamed to reach out for help. Vicarious trauma is not a sign of weakness; it simply reflects that you have empathetically engaged with empathy with your clients. Everyone who works with survivors of trauma is impacted; it is a matter of degree.

2. Engage in self-care activities and plan for this BEFORE you are impacted.
   a. Take care of your physical being through the basics of sleeping enough, eating nutritiously, and getting regular exercise.
   b. Take care of your emotional and interpersonal needs by structuring fun on a regular basis, whether that is through hobbies, music, dance, movies, nature, caring for pets, enjoying or creating art, or having time with family and friends.
   c. Develop and maintain a spiritual practice and/or explore mindfulness meditation.
   d. Engage in professional self-care that includes a range of activities such as regular debriefing with colleagues, a buddy system with a colleague, peer supervision and consultation, ensuring you have a realistic case load (addressing this at an organizational level may be necessary), and taking real breaks; vacations are not a luxury but a necessity.

To work with clients who have experienced trauma, providers must find ways to sustain themselves. Not everyone will find the same approach is helpful and throughout your life and career some strategies will be more helpful than others. As is evident from the list above there are numerous strategies for taking care of oneself. While some will find it restorative to play and laugh while experiencing a favorite hobby or activity, or enjoying the outdoors, others will find restoration in mindfulness and meditation. Having friends or mentors to confide in is a meaningful step in developing self-care. Making sure to get exercise is another strategy, walking, running, dancing, wherever one is comfortable. Listening to music, refraining from using electronic devices, bringing beauty in your environment through artwork, flowers or candles all are possible ways practitioners may sustain themselves.

As part of the graduate curriculum at Lesley University, the participants learned about mindfulness and had opportunities to develop their own practice. Almost without exception participants in the program found the practice of mindfulness to be a particularly helpful addition to their plan for self-care and many have incorporated it into their services with clients. Kabat-Zinn (2005) defined mindfulness as "moment-to-moment, non-judgmental awareness, cultivated by paying attention in a specific way, that is, in the present moment, and as non-reactively, as non-judgmentally, and as openheartedly as possible" (p. 108).

Mindfulness draws upon centuries old practices of meditation of many religious groups. Through the work of Kabat-Zinn and countless others it has been demystified and introduced into secular culture in a way that makes it accessible to all. At the University of Massachusetts Medical School in the early 1980's Kabat-Zinn drew upon meditation practices for severely and chronically ill pain patients who had been deemed almost untreatable, and developed what is now referred to as the Mindfulness Based Stress Reduction (MBSR) program. The MBSR program has grown and been adapted for many populations and contexts and spurred extensive research globally as well as an international embrace of mindfulness practice in sectors as broad ranging as healthcare, business, education, law enforcement and government. Articles about mindfulness are now found on the front cover of popular magazines and showcased on mainstream media. Suffice it to say that the secular practice of mindfulness meditation has become wide spread and no longer viewed as a religious or new age phenomenon. In terms of its relevance to self-care for providers many have found it an invaluable addition to their repertoire.

We encourage professionals to incorporate mindfulness practice into their own self-care. There are a plethora of books and free online apps that are easily accessible. For example Insight Timer can be loaded onto a smart phone and this provides a myriad of guided mindfulness meditations available 24/7. Practitioners can also incorporate this practice into their workshops, preparing others to experience these benefits, whether other colleagues, parents, or young people.

Links to Vicarious Trauma Resources:

http://www.istss.org/treating-trauma/self-care-for-providers.aspx
http://www.headington-institute.org/topic-areas/125/
trauma-and-critical-incidents/246/vicarious-trauma
http://www.joyfulheartfoundation.org/learn/vicarious-trauma

Links to Mindfulness Resources:

http://www.umassmed.edu/cfm/stress-reduction/
https://www.mindandlife.org/

Chapter V: Background on the Lesley University/Guyana Trauma Training Partnership

Forming Our Collaboration

A unique partnership between Lesley University, Graduate School of Arts and Social Sciences, Global Interdisciplinary Studies; UNICEF Guyana; and The Government of Guyana, Ministry of Education and Ministry of Social Services created the Interdisciplinary Master of Arts degree focusing on trauma sensitive assessment and intervention for children, families, and communities. The experiences and insights of the graduates of this program form the basis for this Resource Book.

The Lesley University/Guyana Interdisciplinary Graduate Program began with conversations among individuals who cared about making a difference; specifically, making a difference for the youth of Guyana. Out of those conversations grew a vision and from that vision an invitation; an invitation for Lesley University to develop and deliver a program designed to equip practitioners to address the needs of traumatized youth, families and communities. A key partner in the evolving vision was Ms. Audrey Michele Rodrigues, Learning and Development Officer at UNICEF Guyana. Ms. Rodrigues, who from the outset saw the tremendous potential of this program to impact the wellbeing of children and youth in Guyana, was instrumental in getting UNICEF Guyana's commitment to cost sharing for the two-year period. Throughout the project Ms. Rodrigues played a key role in bringing this remarkable partnership to fruition and was a source of support and encouragement for all.

The Margaret Clemmons Foundation's (MCF) role was pivotal in sparking those initial conversations that led to the invitation. In fact it was Margaret Clemmons herself who first introduced Minister Priya Manickchand of Guyana to the Lesley University community. Both Margaret Clemmons and Minister Manickchand together with a small group visited the Lesley University Cambridge campus in 2009 and were impressed by the integration of expressive arts into our pedagogy and the intersection with social issues. Minister Manickchand was especially committed to addressing the impact of violence upon the youth of Guyana.

Guyanese Highlands

From the beginning, Lesley University was committed to designing a program that would be tailor-made for the needs of youth, families, and communities in Guyana. We conducted two visits to Guyana, the first in 2010 by Associate Provost Gene Diaz and Professor Mitchell Kossak. The Margaret Clemmons Foundation funded this trip. The visit included interviews with a wide range of stakeholders such as leadership from agencies that included private schools, a domestic violence shelter, medical clinics, and the US Embassy. Based upon this a preliminary proposal was developed. A second trip was planned, this time by Dean Catherine Koverola and Associate Provost Gene Diaz. During this second listening tour Koverola and Diaz met with key stakeholders that included supervisors of child welfare and school counseling agencies in Guyana, potential program participants, as well as university administrators at the University of Guyana.

Several key themes and needs emerged in the course of the second visit. It was readily apparent that there was strong consensus that a vast number of social service providers as well as school counselors were ill equipped to deal with the pressing needs of traumatized children, youth, families, and communities. Stakeholders identified serious health and mental health issues that were going unanswered: suicide, sexual abuse, domestic violence, rape, and witness to homicide, as well as anxiety, depression, behavior problems, family dysfunction, truancy, learning problems, bullying, and substance abuse, among others. What also became apparent was that those providing services were significantly impacted in adverse ways by the demands of their work, as they felt overwhelmed and inadequately trained to respond. During our sessions with these stakeholders the sense of relief was palpable among participants as we began to share of the possibility of developing a low residency program at Lesley that would enable individuals from Guyana to gain graduate level skills in assessment and intervention to address these very pressing problems. It was during this initial planning process that the encouragement and support of Ms. Rodrigues was critical.

During our visit to Guyana we had meetings with senior administrators at the University of Guyana and this revealed that at the present time there were no faculty or programs specifically equipped to provide the kind of graduate level educational opportunity that was available at Lesley. This was a very important piece of our assessment, as it would have been highly inappropriate to develop a graduate program from the US if an appropriate one already existed in country.

Following this second visit the Graduate School of Arts and Social Sciences (GSASS) at Lesley University developed an interdisciplinary curriculum drawing from three main fields: Counseling and Psychology, Expressive Arts Therapy, and Mindfulness Studies. The program was designed for practitioners who were working with traumatized youth, families and communities. The curriculum would be culturally relevant and practice focused and committed to taking theory to practice very quickly. The design built upon the skill sets the students would have upon beginning the program. We envisioned that the graduates of the program would be equipped to bring improved counseling and support services to both urban and rural communities in Guyana. Further, by leveraging and building on existing skills, graduates would be empowered to help significantly reduce violence and trauma in Guyana.

In Guyana, as in many developing countries, violence against women and children is endemic. The resulting trauma perpetuates the cycle and has devastating psychological effects, especially on children. This degree program would build the capacity of those offering protection and welfare support services to meet the pressing needs of Guyana's youths. Graduates would emerge not only as skilled mental health practitioners, but also as strong community leaders equipped to train others in their respective organizations and fields.

The Planning team designed a cohort model spanning two years, including two 3-week summer residencies at Lesley University in Cambridge, Massachusetts and two one-week winter residencies in Georgetown, Guyana. Students would continue to develop their work in an online learning environment, while applying their learning to their own professional practice in schools and community agencies.

A Focus on Practical Applications

The program was designed so that students would gain the following competencies:

- Trauma sensitive assessment and counseling skills to address the needs of children, adolescents, and families presenting a range of issues that include: history of trauma and/or victimization,

56

depression, aggression, anxiety, suicide, substance use, crises, loss, learning problems, school adjustment and behavioral problems

- The ability to apply expressive therapies and mindfulness in the delivery of services to children and adolescents including their parents, families, and communities
- The ability to assist classroom teachers on how to design maximally supportive learning environments for children who present with emotional and behavioral distress
- The ability to deliver workshops, trainings, and support groups for parents and community members in order to enhance the capacity of families in caring for their children
- The ability to serve as a leader/mentor/trainer within the community of child mental health service practitioners in Guyana
- The capacity to implement a realistic self-care plan that ensures the prevention of vicarious trauma and burnout within themselves

An Emphasis on Cultural Relevance and Community Based Engagement

The curriculum design recognized that the communities of Guyana are culturally diverse, comprised of a range of ethnic, faith-based, and socio-economic populations. By blending western theoretical approaches and interdisciplinary practical applications, we provided opportunities for the students to master a variety of intervention skills and approaches. We envisioned that by using these tools, graduates would then be able to design and implement community programs and clinical treatment plans that meet the specific needs of their communities. In doing so, graduates were equipped to serve as leaders and role models in their respective fields.

In order to ensure that Lesley faculty involved in the delivery of the curriculum had a comprehensive understanding of the cultural issues Dr. Marjorie Jones, a Guyanese native and faculty member at Lesley

University, provided ongoing consultation to faculty as a whole, as well as individually.

In addition to faculty and staff learning about Guyanese culture in order to facilitate cross-cultural exchange we intentionally planned many opportunities for the students to gain an understanding of western culture by building in opportunities to visit and explore historical and cultural sites/events in the Cambridge/Boston area and engagement with domestic students while they were on campus. We also planned for opportunities to visit many service delivery agencies, particularly ones serving traumatized youth and families. Faculty wove the connection between history and cultural relevance throughout the curriculum.

The program began with the first summer residency in August 2012, and concluded with all thirteen practitioners graduating in May 2014.

The delivery of this program involved a multi-faceted committed team. Faculty involved in the teaching and mentoring included: Sharlene Cochrane, Marjorie Jones, Catherine Koverola, Marion Nesbit, Nancy Waring, Laurie Cozad, Dicki Macy, Robert Macy, Yousef AlAjarma, Deb Spragg, Angelica Pinna-Perez and Vanessa Prosper. Key staff and administrators who supported the project throughout included: Sandra Walker, Lisa Lombardi, Jeffrey Ansloos, and Craig Garland as well as our incredibly supportive team of librarians, including Abby Mancini, Elizabeth Allen, Kathy Holmes, and Dianne Brown.

Bibliography

Chavez, Vivien (2012) *Cultural humility: People, practices, and principles.* https://www.youtube.com/watch?v=SaSHLbS1V4w

Gallardo, Miguel E. ed. (2014) *Developing cultural humility: Embracing race, privilege and power.* Los Angeles: Sage.

Hartwell, C. (2011) https://www.youtube.com/watch?v=QmVvSjQjoBk

Hook, J. N., Davis, D. E., Owen, J., Worthington Jr., E. L., & Utsey, S. O. (2013). Cultural humility: Measuring openness to culturally diverse clients. *Journal of Counseling Psychology®.* Doi: 10.1037/a0032595

Jones, N. A., & Bullock, J. (2012) *The two or more races population: 2010* (PDF, 2.23MB). 2010 Census Briefs. http://www.census.gov/prod/cen2010/briefs/c2010br-13.pdf

Kabot-Zinn, J. (2005). *Coming to our senses: Healing ourselves and the world through mindfulness.* New York: Hyperion.

Pearlman, L.A. & McCann, L. (1990). Vicarious traumatization: A framework for understanding the psychological effects of working with victims. *Journal of Traumatic Stress,* Vol. 3, No. 1.

Pearlman, L.A. & Saakvitne, K.W. (1995) *Trauma and the Therapist: Countertransference and Vicarious Traumatization in Psychotherapy with Incest Survivors.* New York: W.W. Norton.

Rosen, D.C. (2014). Beyond Dualities: Navigating Privilege and Marginalization as a Multicultural Psychologist, in Gallardo, Miguel

E. ed. *Developing cultural humility: Embracing race, privilege and power.* Los Angeles: Sage.

Seecharan, C. (1997). Culture and ethnicity in post-emancipation Guyana. *Slavery & Abolition,* 18:2, 128-138. DOI: 10.1080/01440399708575214

Tervalon, M., & Murray-Garcia, J. (1998). Cultural humility versus cultural competence: A critical distinction in defining physician-training outcomes in multicultural education. *Journal of Health Care for the Poor and Underserved,* 9, 117-125.

Trotz, (2003). *Behind the Banner of Culture? Gender, Race, and the Family in Guyana* http://www.jstor.org.gate2.library.lse.ac.uk/stable/pdf/41850226.pdf

Waters, A., Asbill, L. (2013). Reflections on cultural humility. *APA Newsletter.*
http://apa.org/pi/families/resources/newsletter/2013/08/cultural-humility.aspx

The World Factbook 2013-14. Washington, DC: Central Intelligence Agency, 2013.
https://www.cia.gov/library/publications/the-world-factbook/geos/gy.html

World Life Expectancy (2014)
http://www.worldlifeexpectancy.com/cause-of-death/suicide/by-country/

http://www.worldlifeexpectancy.com/cause-of-death/violence/by-country/

Author Biographies

Sharlene Voogd Cochrane
Dr. Cochrane, Professor Emeritus, has over thirty years experience in education, specifically with adults returning to college and master's degree students in courses and independent studies. She also serves as a senior advisor in the Ph.D. in Educational Studies Program. Her research and exploration in the cultural implications of curriculum and pedagogy has shaped her teaching, primarily within the Lesley University Graduate School of Arts and Social Sciences. She has served as Dean of Faculty responsible for faculty development across the four schools of the University. Her roles in the Lesley/Guyana Program included serving as faculty advisor for the students, teaching courses, and guiding their thesis projects. She is a contributing author and co-editor of the recently published book, *Culturally Responsive Teaching and Learning in Higher Education: Promising Practices From the Cultural Literacy Curriculum Institute* (2017). The Institute, which she helped to establish and facilitate, provides a professional development opportunity for faculty to develop curriculum and pedagogy related to cultural literacy.

Marjorie A. Jones
Dr. Marjorie Jones, Professor Emeritus, has taught courses in education, with specific responsibility for middle and high school teacher education programs, humanities and social science, and is a Senior Advisor in the Ph.D. in Educational Studies Program. She has served as the chair of the Lesley University Diversity Council. In the Lesley/Guyana program she served as 'Cultural Consultant' to inform both content and pedagogy, working directly with faculty and students. She is Guyanese by birth and served at the University of Guyana as Senior Lecturer, Head: Department of Foundations and Administration, Dean-Faculty

of Education, Deputy Vice-Chancellor, and Director of Development. She has done extensive work in curriculum development and served as the chair of the curriculum committee that developed the medical program in Guyana. She is a contributing author and co-editor of the recently published book, *Culturally Responsive Teaching and Learning in Higher Education: Promising Practices From the Cultural Literacy Curriculum Institute* (2017).

Catherine Koverola

Dr. Catherine Koverola, currently Provost at Cambridge College, is a leader in higher education administration. A program innovator she has led the development of many interdisciplinary graduate programs across the globe. Dr. Koverola is a clinical psychologist with over 20 years of experience as a clinician, having provided services to a wide range of populations domestically and internationally. As both an educator and clinician she has been a pioneer in the ever-evolving advances of the integration of technology in education and tele-medicine; exploring innovative approaches to ensure access particularly to those most marginalized in society. The focus of her clinical work has been in the domains of child abuse, victimization, suicide, and vicarious traumatization of providers. She has unique expertise in the delivery of services in remote and rural communities and has developed culturally relevant programs that serve victims of violence in locations as varied as urban medical centers to remote indigenous communities. Dr. Koverola is an internationally recognized scholar in the area of interpersonal victimization in cross-cultural contexts, and she also writes on emerging issues in higher education.